WHY NOT WASTE TIME WITH GOD?

Group Study Workbook

BY MICHAEL EVANS

WITH CARLA KLEIVER

Archer-Ellison Publishing Company
Winter Park, Florida

2

TABLE OF CONTENTS

KEY POINTS

In the following outlines the underlined words are suggested words to be left blank when outlines are used as fill-in handouts.

1

WAITING AND WASTING

The introduction to this chapter compares how God feels about time with you with how you feel about time with your <u>child.</u>

WAITING IS HARD

- Dutch Sheets: "We do not wait well. We're into microwaving. God, on the other hand, is usually into <u>marinating</u>."
- We are well acquainted with doing things <u>for</u> God, rather than sitting <u>with</u> Him and doing nothing.
- Thomas Kelly: "…in guilty regret we must postpone till next week that deeper life of unshaken composure in the holy Presence, where we sincerely know our true home is, for this week is much too <u>full</u>."

WHY WOULD WE WANT TO WAIT?

- Waiting brings about this nagging feeling that we are being <u>selfish.</u>
- This misplaced guilt is from a misunderstanding: We do not fully <u>know</u> the God with whom we are spending time!
- He <u>wants</u> to waste time with us! (Isaiah 40:31; 30:18)
- He calls us to come out and be <u>separate</u> (2 Corinthians 6:17- 7:1); to come away from the rat race of the world.
- Edward Schillebeeckx: "Failure to recognize the value of mere being with God, as the beloved, without doing anything, is to gouge the <u>heart</u> out of Christianity."

CATCHING THE WAVES

- People have <u>misconceptions</u> about prolonged times with the Lord
    1. For super spiritual giants of times past – "I could never do that!"
    2. We think it sounds like Eastern Mysticism or New Age.
    3. We believe it is not as important as doing something for God.
- Instead we rush to the latest book, conference or workshop – from one <u>wave</u> to the other.
- Brennan Manning: "Have you ever felt baffled by your internal resistance to prayer? By the … <u>dread</u> of silence, solitude and being alone with God?"
- We dread being alone with God because it requires a level of intimacy we <u>fear.</u>

INTIMACY

- Intimacy requires transparency and <u>risk</u>.
- Intimacy denotes relationship with a close <u>friend.</u>
- C. Raymond Beran: [With a true friend] "You do not have to be on your guard. With him you breath freely…You do not have to be careful…He understands…Through it all – and underneath – he sees, knows and loves you…What is a friend? Just one…with whom you dare be yourself."
- When I understand that He <u>accepts</u> me, then I can begin to grasp my uniqueness and destiny as a child of eternity.

FROM FIERY PASSION TO SMOLDERING ASHES

- The passion we had when we first became Christians eventually <u>dies</u>, and we feel we've fallen from God and His love.
- Some of us <u>compare</u> ourselves with other believers or with a standard of performance (I should witness, I should obey God's rules, etc.)
- We have both a burning desire to please the Lord and "a <u>fear</u> that whatever we are doing isn't quite good enough."
- How do we turn this extrinsic motivation (motivation outside ourselves to do things) into intrinsic motivation (motivation from <u>within</u>)?

IMPEDIMENTS TO INTIMACY

- What often hinders our intimacy with God is the same thing that hinders our intimacy with <u>people</u>.
- *"Doing"* – Living out in the power of the flesh what was started in the power of the <u>Spirit</u> (Galatians 3:1-3).
- *Fearing Rejection* – Trying to keep from God the truth about ourselves, that we are "a tangled mass of <u>fears</u> and frustrations."
    1. But God desires to go beneath the surface to the <u>real</u> person living inside our skin.
    2. We are like the leper in Mark 1:40 who has been <u>rejected</u> by everyone (including himself) and is afraid Jesus may reject him, too.
    3. Henri Nouwen: "Self-rejection is the greatest enemy of the spiritual life because it contradicts the sacred voice that calls us the '<u>Beloved</u>'."

4. God will never reject us…He will always reach across the chasm that separates us and will embrace us (See Luke 15.)
- *Walking in Darkness* – John 1:5-10
     1. It is not allowing God's light to reveal the truth about any area of our lives not <u>surrendered</u> to Him.
     2. Walking in darkness is not being <u>honest</u> with God, and intimacy is rooted in honesty.

RECOVERING INTIMACY

- *Giving up the "Doing"* – God Himself, not your performance, is <u>responsible</u> for your spiritual growth (Philippians 1:6)
- *Overcoming Rejection* – It begins with ruthless, naked <u>trust</u>.
     1. Thomas Merton: "Surrender your poverty and acknowledge your nothingness to the Lord."
     2. Surrender your plans, dreams, feelings and attitudes about life.
     3. Yes, God already <u>knows</u> all there is to know about you, but when you, by a direct act of the <u>will</u>, choose to expose and surrender those areas to God, you are freeing yourself from the <u>burden</u> of guilt and shame.
     4. There comes a time when we cannot say we love God and <u>exclude</u> Him from the real person inside this flesh…If we confess whatever it is in us that keeps us from the intimacy we were created to experience, forgiveness is immediate.
- *Walking in the Light* – Intimacy requires that we be vulnerable…and <u>accountable</u> (I John 1:7,8).

WAITING ON GOD

- Waiting before the Lord in <u>silence</u> gives God time and space to lead, to tell us how to pray and what to pray.
- Why would you ask God to give you an answer on something and then not <u>wait</u> for Him to give it!

WASTING TIME WITH HIM

- Why is it necessary? What are the benefits?
     1. <u>Peace</u>, settledness in your spirit
     2. Growing realization of how <u>special</u> you are to Him
     3. Growing realization that God's approval does not depend on what you do or do not do
     4. Lessening of fears about the <u>future</u>
     5. Lessening of dependence on others for <u>approval</u>
     6. Increasing enjoyment of solitude and <u>silence</u>
     7. Increasing appreciation of the world around you
     8. Seeing others with <u>new</u> eyes
     9. New and fresh <u>passion</u> for God
     10. More compassionate love
     11. Freer giving of yourself

12. Taking yourself less <u>seriously</u>
13. Pretense and striving for approval are replaced by <u>confidence</u> that you are significant, accepted and loved.

- Prepare yourself to waste time with God.

Discussion questions for this chapter are on page 56

2

THE VALUE OF NURTURING THE SOUL

The introduction to this chapter points out that most of us do long for and pant for something, but not for <u>God</u>, and yet the very thing we need in order to speak and act from strength and peace is a nurturing relationship with God.

WHAT WE SEE IN THE MIRROR
- Many of us struggle with accepting ourselves and our flaws, and we assume that Jesus does not accept us either.
- David Seamonds: "Satan's greatest psychological weapon is a feeling of ... low <u>self-worth</u>."

TREASURE IN JARS OF CLAY
- Though we are like cracked and imperfect jars made of clay, Paul writes that there is a priceless <u>treasure</u> within us (2 Corinthians 4:7).
- The treasure is the <u>power </u>of the living God.
- When God looks at us, He looks past the flaws and sees the treasure.
- Without an intimate, nurturing relationship with God, we cannot <u>grasp</u> what a treasure God deposited in us.
- Story of the two water pots: God uses what we see as flaws to bring life and <u>beauty</u> to those around us.

GOD MADE US OF IMMENSE WORTH AND VALUE

- The Bible affirms that human beings are valuable (1 Peter 2:9-10), created in God's <u>image</u>.
- Charles Kraft writes about two valuable capabilities of humans of which Satan is jealous:
  1. The ability to <u>procreate</u> physically: Although the image of God in us has been marred, "we can still say that we are made in His image and have been given the privilege by God to procreate others in His image."
  2. The potential (if we allow God) to be <u>transformed</u> in His image spiritually: "If you received God's seed (DNA) it will cause you to become more like Him."
- More evidence of our value in God's sight: We have been placed in a position to <u>rule</u> over all creation (Genesis 1:26,27 and Psalms 8:6-8).
- He formed you (Jeremiah 1:5) and He <u>likes</u> what He formed!
- Do you think God would have sent His only Son to die for us if we were not <u>special</u>?
- God knows we are ungodly and helpless, but that does <u>not</u> mean we are unredeemable and worthless.

WE MISUNDERSTAND LOVE

- Loving ourselves is not a form of <u>pride</u>.
- Loving ourselves is a grateful dependence on God and a realistic appraisal of both our strengths and weaknesses.
- We are like candles (author unknown): "We have all it takes to be human beings. Yet we need a gift, a spark of <u>love</u> from our God. Then we glow."
- We must not make light of our sinfulness and our need to be cleansed by the blood of Jesus, but God wants an intimate relationship with us. He wants us to come before Him so He can <u>forgive</u> us.

RESULTS OF A POOR SELF-IMAGE

- *A Lack of Trust* – We look at ourselves, whose image we despise, and <u>overlook</u> what God is preparing to accomplish in and through our lives.
- *Rebellion* – We feel cheated; we see Him as an <u>authority</u> figure who has wronged us and consequently resent other authority figures.
- *Inability to Build Genuine Relationships* – We are so oversensitive to the response others have to our appearance or abilities, we become unable to concentrate on <u>their</u> real needs.
- *Seeking Acceptance and Approval* – We overemphasize clothes or possessions to cover up rejection of self, or we perform and accomplish (a human "<u>doing</u>" instead of a human "being"), or we try to get <u>approval</u> from God through spiritual activity, or we even do bad things to at least get noticed.
- *Negative Body or Mind Image-* We have <u>negative</u> feelings toward our bodies or minds, especially the parts of us that do not line up with what the media says we should have.
- *A Sense of Shame* – We may sense shame for even existing and use a variety of behaviors to <u>cover</u> our shame, such as alcohol, drugs, sex or even religion.
- *Cursing Ourselves* – We may direct <u>hateful</u> words toward ourselves or parts of our bodies.

WE ARE AT WAR!

- A poor self-image and all of the accompanying beliefs are simply <u>lies</u>.
- <u>Satan</u> uses the lies and whatever other means he has available to defeat and destroy us.

FIGHTING THE BATTLE

- *Claim protection* – This includes avoiding places where your worth and value are constantly <u>attacked</u>, unless you are sent there by God as an ambassador of Christ.
- *Know Who You Are in Christ*
  1. <u>None</u> of us is a mistake. Conception is not simply a physical, human act. Only God can give the life that courses through our physical bodies.
  2. Neil Anderson: In <u>Christ</u>, we are accepted (John 1:12), secure (Romans 8:35), and significant (Ephesians 2:10).
- Do Not Focus on Circumstances
  1. We are apt to think that circumstances <u>control</u> us, but we can rise above them.
  2. Neil Anderson: "If you see yourself as a child of God who is spiritually alive in Christ, you'll begin to live in <u>victory</u> and freedom."
- *Renew Your Mind*
  1. Pull down strongholds and fortresses of thought patterns and bring each thought into <u>captivity</u> to Christ (2 Corinthians 10:4-5).
  2. Replace those thoughts with biblically based thoughts, thinking God's <u>truth</u> (Philippians 4:8).
- *Wait in Silence* – "Silence" in Psalm 62 comes from the Hebrew word for "whisper softly", indicating that we must wait, expecting God <u>only</u> to speak to us in a way that no one else can hear.

A NURTURING RELATIONSHIP

- Such a relationship
  1. Allows us to speak and act from <u>strength</u> rather than from fear or insecurity.
  2. Enables us to truly understand our true value and <u>worth</u>.
  3. Helps us to be comfortable sitting quietly in His <u>presence</u>.
- If you want to love God above all else in the world, you must <u>nurture</u> your relationship with Him.

Discussion questions for this chapter are on page 57

3

THE BENEFITS OF WAITING ON GOD

The introduction to this chapter reviews the well-known story of King Saul's impatience. He was commanded to <u>wait</u> and he did not wait (1 Samuel 13). It shows how humans have always tended to take matters into their own hands rather than wait on God, obey Him without fear or question, and trust Him as their <u>provider</u>.

SCRIPTURE TEACHES THAT GOD IS OUR PROVIDER

- God provided <u>everything</u> the Israelites needed in the desert after they escaped Egypt.
- Jesus tells us not to worry. God <u>knows</u> what we need, and that as we make His kingdom and righteousness our priority, our needs will be provided (Matthew 6:28-34).

GOD'S PROVISION FOR ABRAHAM

- God <u>tested</u> Abraham by asking him to sacrifice his son Isaac (Genesis 22:1-13).
- Isaac did not know he was the sacrifice, so on the way to the place of sacrifice, he asked his father, "<u>Where</u> is the lamb for the offering?"
- Abraham said, "God himself will <u>provide</u> the lamb."
- Think of what both father and son were experiencing emotionally as Abraham finally laid his only son on the altar and prepared to kill him.
- Abraham was at the most desperate, lowest point of his life, brought about as a result of his covenant and obedience to God. But he <u>trusted</u> that somehow God would bring his son back to him.

- Abraham did not know why God wanted him to do this thing, but the important point is that he <u>did</u> it! Only then, as Abraham stood poised with the knife in his hand, did God <u>stop</u> him and provide a lamb for the sacrifice.
- Will God, as our <u>provider</u>, do any less for us?

OUR NEEDS ARE NO SURPRISE TO GOD

- Nothing "<u>occurs</u>" to God. He knows what we need.
- God: You are talking to ME. So what's the <u>problem</u>?

MY OWN JOURNEY OF FAITH IN MY PROVIDER

- It is easy to talk about faith and trust and to walk in it for short periods of time. But over the long haul God begins to dig deep into our very souls and expose those areas of our lives that want to be in <u>control</u>.
- Burnout in the middle of 2000 led to taking a sabbatical.
- During this time I began to <u>examine</u> and deal with some things about myself that I did not want to face.
- I had to deal with my own trust in God, faith in God, and even my blatant and childish <u>ungratefulness</u> for what God had done in the past and was doing in the present.

WE ARE OFTEN UNGRATEFUL

- The Israelites: "<u>If only</u> we had meat to eat! … We never see anything but this manna" (Numbers 11:4-6).
- Moses: "I cannot carry all these people by myself… If this is how you are going to treat me, put me to <u>death</u> right now" (Numbers 11:10-15).
- God: "Now the Lord will <u>give</u> you meat…until you <u>loathe</u> it" (Numbers 11:18-20).
- We do not trust in God, and then we go one step farther and <u>complain</u> about what He does provide for us.

LEARNED TO WAIT

- During this time when I hit the wall, I literally could do <u>nothing</u> but wait for God.
- 1,000 dollars were needed at this time to print the Hungarian edition of my book.
- "God is going to have to <u>drop</u> it in my hands in the next 24 hours."
- A man came for prayer and two hours later he put ten 100 dollar bills in my <u>hand</u>.

SILENCE AND STILLNESS EQUAL REST

- When we come to realize that God is <u>responsible</u> for us and that He will provide, then we understand how important it is to "waste time with Him."
- Waiting becomes <u>healing</u> to us.
- Francis Frangipane: "Many leaders have worked themselves to exhaustion seeking to serve God. If they spent half their time with Him, in prayer and waiting before Him, they would find His <u>supernatural</u> accompaniment working mightily in their efforts."

- Brennan Manning: "Silence is not simply the absence of noise...but rather a process of coming to <u>stillness</u>. Silent solitude forges true speech. I'm not speaking of physical isolation: solitude here means being alone with the <u>Alone</u>, experiencing the transcendent Other and growing in <u>awareness</u> of one's identity as the <u>beloved</u>."
- Once we sit still in silence with Him we will know true <u>peace</u> and rest.
- The Sabbath was not a source of rest for God. It was a source of rest for <u>man</u>.
- Fulfillment is found when we spend time with Him and <u>cease</u> our pitiful efforts for His approval.
- It is <u>okay</u> with God for us to just be ourselves, for He loves us and wants us to be with Him even though we are doing absolutely <u>nothing</u> but enjoying His Presence.
- When I get up, I pour myself a cup of coffee, sit quietly in a comfortable chair and <u>listen</u> for God to speak to me.
- If we go before God and ask Him to <u>speak</u> to us, why are we so surprised when He actually does!
- Father Ammons: "I have shown you the power of silence, how thoroughly it heals and how fully <u>pleasing</u> it is to God."
- It is that very silence and stillness that not only contributes to our <u>nurture</u> but is healing to our souls and spirits.

Discussion questions for this chapter are on page 58

4

ARE YOU LISTENING?

The introduction to this chapter introduces another component to waiting on God. In addition to sitting in solitude and silence before God, we must learn how to <u>listen</u> to Him.

PRAYER INVOLVES LISTENING

- Prayer is <u>conversation</u> with God.
- Though conversation involves listening, we are not very good at it.
    1.   We are thinking of what we will say in response.
    2.   Our own <u>agenda</u> causes us to listen to what we want to hear and ignore what does not fit with what we want.
- We have the same listening problems in our conversation with <u>God</u>.
    1. When an answer from Him does not correspond with what we <u>want</u> to do, we go back to Him and talk it over.
    2. Assuming we have His blessing, we move <u>ahead</u>, encountering opposition.
    3. Then we blame God for the <u>mess</u>.

BALAAM AND HIS DONKEY

- An example of a man who did not <u>like</u> God's answer (Numbers 22).
- He asked God if he should curse Israel on behalf of King Balak and God said <u>no</u>.
- Even though he had received a very clear answer to his prayer, Balaam decided he would go back and ask <u>again</u>.
- He had been offered money from King Balak.

- He was trying to convince God to <u>change</u> His mind and he was trying to justify his actions.
- Balaam was talking to God, but he was <u>not</u> listening to what God was saying.
- God finally relented and let him go, but He was very <u>angry</u> when Balaam went (Numbers 22:22).
- Wanting to teach Balaam that His no means no, God tried three different times to get Balaam's <u>attention</u> (diversion, physical pain and blocking his path).
- God will use any means <u>necessary</u> – even a donkey- to get our attention and attempt to stop us from doing something foolish.
- If God resorted to something this ridiculous, would you <u>listen</u>?
- If you want to hear His voice, it is imperative that you wait, <u>listen</u> and obey.
- If we persist in going our own way, often He will bring <u>opposition</u> to try and turn us from our disobedience.
- When we go to God to sit and listen, we must go with no <u>agenda</u> or preconceived ideas of what we expect to hear.
- When we lay our requests before Him and listen to Him, His cleansing fire will reveal to us our motives, which could keep us from making costly <u>mistakes</u>.

DISCERNING THE VOICE OF GOD

- David is called "a man after God's own <u>heart</u>."
- This did not stem from David's perfection, but from the fact that David longed to do God's will with all his heart. He wanted to <u>hear</u> from God.
- David grew in his discernment of God's <u>voice</u>.
- As we grow in the use of discernment we become more adept at <u>recognizing</u> the voice of God (See 1 Corinthians 2:14 and Hebrews 5:14).
- Three voices vie for our attention: our own, God's and <u>Satan's</u>.
- God's voice is always <u>positive</u>, affirming, corrective, encouraging and unrushed.
- Satan's voice is negative, <u>condemning</u>, discouraging, and often calling for impulsive or hurried behavior.
- We must learn not only how to <u>sort</u> through our own thoughts but also the lies, temptations or other distractions that the enemy plants in our minds.
- The more <u>intimate</u> your relationship is with the Lord, the easier it will be for you to recognize His voice.

GOD IS TRYING TO GET YOUR ATTENTION

- Often, we can discern the voice of God without even <u>realizing</u> it.
- Example: Years ago, the word "kneecap" came into my mind at the end of a worship service, and the Lord prompted me to go to the microphone and ask if anyone was having a problem with his or her knee. A person came forward, God revealed further that there was a hairline fracture in his kneecap, which the man confirmed was true. We prayed for the man and he was <u>healed</u>.
- Later, a wiser and more experienced Christian told me that I had received words of <u>knowledge</u> from the Lord.

An Exercise in Listening to the Voice of God

- This is an exercise I have groups do when I speak on the subject of listening to God.
    1. Break into small groups of three people who do <u>not</u> know each other.
    2. Do not introduce yourselves or <u>reveal</u> any information about yourselves.
    3. Close your eyes and be <u>silent</u> and still.
    4. When everyone is ready to begin, I pray that God will <u>reveal</u> to each person in the room something specific that He wants him or her to pray for someone in the group.
    5. What God reveals may have to do with physical pain, a family problem, a relationship, emotional distress or a spiritual problem.
    6. Without fail, eighty-five percent of the people report that God <u>gave</u> them a word or picture concerning someone in their group.
- "There is no way you could have known that unless God <u>revealed</u> it to you!"

Two Areas of Discernment

- Discernment of God's <u>truth</u>
    1. It is imperative that we both listen to instruction in God's <u>Word</u> and spend time studying and dividing the Word of Truth for ourselves (See 2 Timothy 2:15 and 2 Timothy 3:16-17).
    2. The Spirit reveals to us how the Word <u>applies</u> in any given place or time.
    3. The same scripture may be used at different times with <u>differing</u> applications to our circumstances.
    4. Discernment is for this moment, when a passage you have read before will come to life in a <u>new</u> way and fit the unique circumstance in which you find yourself.
- Discernment of God's direction, guidance and information for us personally
    1. God <u>communicates</u> through thoughts, mental pictures, other people, nature, visions, dreams, etc.
    2. We must be wise in how we <u>apply</u> what we are hearing or seeing.
    3. The message must not <u>contradict</u> God's Word.
    4. When someone comes to you with a prophetic word from the Lord, you must take it to God in prayer and ask that He <u>confirm</u> it, because it is wise to make sure that God is the One speaking.

Discernment Comes From Choosing to Listen

- Jesus: "My sheep <u>listen</u> to My voice; I know them and they <u>follow</u> Me" (John 10:27).
- He expects us to learn to know His <u>voice</u> in our thoughts.
- We can shut these thoughts down if we <u>choose</u>.

THE DISCERNED WORD MUST COINCIDE WITH SCRIPTURE

- He will <u>never</u> tell us anything contrary to His written Word.
- We can read other books and seek counsel, but the final decision must <u>line</u> up with what you know to be God's truth.

SLOW DOWN, TUNE OUT THE STATIC AND LISTEN

- "Be <u>still</u> and know that I am God" (Psalm 46:10).
- To walk in true discernment, our hearts must be <u>quiet</u> before God.
- True discernment comes through a heart that has ceased <u>striving</u>, a heart that knows, even in the fiery trial of its personal struggle, that the Lord is God.
- Thoughts and reactions can <u>block</u> us from hearing God, like a jamming station that inhibits our powers of discernment.
- We must <u>die</u> to personal judgments, ideas of retaliation and self-motivation.
- As we stop our striving and <u>listen</u>, we discern (See Psalms 62:2).

Discussion questions for this chapter are on page 59

5

THE TRAGEDY OF THE CHURCH TODAY

The introduction to this chapter conveys the fact that most churches focus on <u>growth</u> and prosperity and lose sight of the simple message of the <u>cross</u>.

LOSING THE MESSAGE OF THE CROSS

- We have so watered down the <u>cost</u> that we have convinced people they can have all the benefits of the Gospel without any inconvenience to their way of life.
- Yet the purpose of a Roman cross was to bring about an end to a human being. When the cross finished its work, the victim was <u>dead</u>.
- The message of the cross is not an improved old life, but an entirely <u>new</u> life.
- Jesus: 'If anyone wishes to come after Me, let him deny himself, and take up his <u>cross</u>, and follow Me" (Matthew 16:24).
- A.W. Tozer: "If we are to truly die upon it [the cross], we must be willing to submit the whole way we live our lives to be <u>destroyed</u> and built again in the power of an endless life."

FINDING SUITABLE TIME IN SOLITUDE WITH GOD

- The words quietness, obedience, discipline, humility, simplicity and suffering are all <u>foreign</u> to our culture.
- Most common response: "I do not have <u>time</u>!"
- We need <u>reformation</u> as individuals and as the corporate Church.
- A.W. Tozer: "To beg for a flood of blessing to come upon a backslidden and disobedient church is a waste of time and effort. God is not interested in increased church <u>attendance</u>, unless those who attend amend their ways and begin to live <u>holy</u> lives."

Religion As An Opiate

- Thomas Merton: "Without a total love of God and an uncompromising <u>thirst</u> for His truth, religion tends in the end to become an opiate."
- According to the dictionary, an opiate is "something that <u>dulls</u> the senses and induces relaxation."
- So religion can actually dull our spiritual sense and put us in a state where we are <u>happy</u> with the status quo.
- For much of the Church, religion is a dull <u>habit</u>.

Why Do We Settle?

- Why do we settle for life at a level that is so much <u>less</u> than what God intends for us?
- Brennan Manning: "We sometimes settle for less because we are <u>cowards</u>."
- Part of the reason that we are so content in the shallows is because it is <u>safe</u>.
- We are contented with a snack, and yet there is a complete <u>feast</u> awaiting us.
- We do not know by experience the precious, consuming presence of the <u>Spirit</u> of God.

From the Shallows to the Depths

- A.W. Tozer: "Are you sure that you want to be possessed by a Spirit Who, while He is pure and gentle and wise and loving, will yet insist upon being <u>Lord</u> of your life?"
- This wholehearted surrender will not only transform our lives, but it also will <u>radically</u> change the face of the Church.

God Calls Us to Much More Than Normal

- There is no limit to what He can do, but <u>*we*</u> can limit what He can do in, with and through *us*.
- God will not violate our will. He will <u>allow</u> us to be status quo Christians if that is what we want.
- We like familiarity, but staying comfortable with those things that are normal and familiar keeps us from experiencing the <u>extraordinary</u>.
- Francis Frangipane: "God does not want us 'normal,' He wants us to be <u>Christlike</u>!"
- To become Christlike, we must do the things that Christ <u>did</u>!
- God is so deep, so high, so wide, so entirely unfathomable to our finite minds that always we will be challenged to move further <u>away</u> from being comfortable, satisfied and normal. There is nothing normal about God.

Obedience and Humility

- When we begin to spend time with God, He <u>reveals</u> things about us that we do not want to give up – habits, interests, secret vanities, attitudes, and prejudices.
- We must allow Him to reveal to us all those hidden places and be <u>willing</u> to let him change and purify us. This requires obedience and humility.
- Like Jesus, when we move into an intimate relationship with the Father, we will, because

of that relationship, <u>submit</u> ourselves to man.

OBEDIENCE REQUIRES YIELDING

- God places into the Bank of God a deposit that makes each of us a spiritual multimillionaire, but He will not write our checks. He has done His <u>part</u>, and we must do ours.
- Our part is <u>obedience</u>.
- The yield sign – If we are not willing to yield our <u>rights</u> at an intersection, it could cost us our lives.
- Why is it, then, that in our daily lives we go casually along our way without yielding ourselves to what the Father wants to do with us? We behave as if there are no <u>consequences</u>.
- Obedience is the road to intimacy and intimacy comes through <u>yielding</u>. We are not going to be willing to yield to Him if we do not trust Him or understand what yielding involves.
- He only gives as much as we <u>allow</u> Him to give.
- Anonymous quote on a church bulletin: "As Savior He cannot save us from sin we <u>insist</u> upon retaining; as Head of the Body He cannot direct a stubborn member; as Lord He cannot reveal His will to one who does not <u>want</u> to know it or obey it; as Life He cannot fill what is already filled with a totally different substance; as Sanctifier He cannot separate us wholly unto Himself when we <u>prefer</u> to live unto self and the world; as Lord He cannot use us to defeat the enemy when we ourselves have already allowed him to defeat us."

THE YIELDED LIFE

- We do not yield *in order* to be His but <u>because</u> we are His. Our purchase by His blood gives Him title, delivery and possession (See Romans 6:16).
- What the yielded life is <u>not</u>:
    1. Merely holding to a particular belief.
    2. Merely the saving of our souls.
    3. Simply giving oneself to a particular kind of service.
    4. Stopping evil practices.
    5. Merely praying or reading the Bible.
- What the yielded life <u>is</u>: Giving Him our <u>whole</u> selves – our bodies, our members, our being. It includes everything – mind, emotions, will, home, families, possessions, occupation, friendship, time, money, goals, the past, present, future, our worst and our best. It is the glad, joyous <u>willing</u> response of <u>love</u> to love.
- From *Others May, You Cannot* (author unknown): "If God has called you to be really like <u>Jesus</u>, …He will draw you into a life of crucifixion and humility and put on you such demands of obedience that He will not allow you to follow <u>other</u> Christians…Now when you are so possessed with the living God that you are in your secret heart pleased and <u>delighted</u> over this peculiar, personal, private, jealous guardianship and management of

the Holy Spirit over your life, you will have found the vestibule of <u>heaven</u>."

REFUSING TO YIELD

- We cannot just bring the troublesome, unmanageable <u>parts</u> of our lives to God, asking Him for spiritual repairs.
- Example: A man whose clock doesn't work correctly, but brings <u>only</u> the hands to the jeweler and not the whole clock.
- Different reasons for not yielding everything to Him
    1. Hard to believe He can <u>accept</u> us because there is so much bad in our lives.
    2. No problem bringing God the sins, but we see no reason to bring Him the <u>best</u> of ourselves.
    3. We reserve some areas for ourselves and offer <u>substitutes</u>.
- The refusal to yield any part is an act of rebellion and will make it <u>difficult</u> to experience the fullness of the Holy Spirit in our lives.
- This is not an impossible journey, and God does not wait for perfection. Wherever you are in your spiritual walk, if you can begin to submit yourself to Him and spend time with Him, then God will use your <u>whole</u> journey.
- Thomas Kelly: "Don't grit your teeth and clench your fists and say 'I will! I will!' Relax. Take hands off. Submit yourself to God. Learn to live in the passive voice and let life be willed <u>through</u> you. For 'I will' spells not obedience."

MAINTAIN THE MESSAGE

- The message of the cross brings death to our old way of life and brings us into life and power.
- If we, the Corporate Church, are to become a significant force for <u>change</u> in our world, we must declare this message, and the individual members of the Church must <u>live</u> it.

Discussion questions for this chapter are on page 60

6

THE FOOLISHNESS OF GOD

*The introduction to this chapter brings up two spheres of foolishness in the
<u>world's</u> eyes: the built-in "foolishness" of the message of the cross
(1 Corinthians 1:18) and the verdict of foolishness that we Christians bring
upon ourselves because there is so little demonstration of the true <u>power</u> of
God in our lives. But, in spite of what may appear to be foolish to the
world, God's original message and plan have not changed.*

GOD'S MESSAGE AND PLAN

- God's two-part plan
  1. To <u>redeem</u> mankind from the sentence of death and bring us back into intimate relationship with Himself (John 3:16).
  2. To establish a group of people, who after Jesus' death and resurrection, were instructed to take the simple message of the cross to the whole <u>world</u>.
- The message: Redemption from death was given totally by the grace and mercy of God. It is free. We cannot <u>earn</u> it. We are simply His <u>beloved</u>.
- Too good to be true? To the world this "marketing plan" is <u>foolish</u>.
- How would *we* plan to communicate a message to the entire world?
  1. Convene <u>influential</u> people in a corporate boardroom.
  2. Determine how to obtain large amounts of <u>money</u>.
  3. Find the brightest and <u>sharpest</u> people to implement the plan.

4. Contact those with <u>name</u> recognition, power and authority to make things happen.
- For the many "causes" in this world, this strategy works (i.e. Jerry Lewis and Muscular Dystrophy telethon).
- But the Scriptural message we have received and the way in which we are to proclaim it is quite <u>different</u> from this worldly scenario.
- Eugene Peterson in *The Message* (1 Corinthians 1:20-24): "God in his wisdom took delight in using what the world considered dumb – preaching of all things! – to bring those who trust him into the way of salvation… Jews treat this like an anti-miracle, and Greeks pass it off as <u>absurd</u>. But to us who are personally called by God himself – both Jews and Greeks – Christ is God's ultimate miracle and wisdom all wrapped up in one."
- We Christians should be able to see that the <u>worldly</u> messages - the multitude of ways the world believes we can attain health, wealth, peace and prosperity – are foolishness when <u>compared</u> with the message of the cross.

PEACE, MY BROTHER

- I participated in the peace movement of the 60's. It was great at first, but the scene started to turn <u>ugly</u>.
- I was 24, and at the lowest point of my life, emotionally and spiritually. I was 12 when I became a Christian and now 12 years later, I was facing something I could not <u>handle</u>.
- "Lord, if you are there, I need you to show me, and I <u>give</u> myself to you, as much as I know how, to do with as you want."
- I felt this warm wind and was overwhelmed with such a feeling of warmth and <u>peace</u>.
- It was the first step in the journey of <u>learning</u> how to live in God's peace.

GOD'S MESSAGE VS. THE WORLD'S MESSAGE

- The "wisdom of man" - All the various <u>ways</u> offered in the 60's to find peace and tranquility have metamorphosed into other forms in our day and age.
    1. Televangelists promise health and <u>wealth</u>.
    2. Marketing experts tell us life will be more fun and people will like us if we use the right <u>products</u>.
    3. Popular movie personalities espouse <u>New Age</u> pluralism.
    4. Role models, heroes, leaders tell us it is <u>okay</u> to use recreational drugs, engage in illicit sex, have abortions, etc.
- Consider the world's messages against the message of the cross. Which of them sounds the <u>most</u> foolish?
- To human ears, the truths of the Gospel sound like foolishness because
    1. They are <u>simple</u>.
    2. They are equally <u>free</u> to the unlearned and the highly educated.
    3. They <u>set aside</u> self-righteous works.
    4. They offend religious pride because a cross is such a sign of helpless weakness that it seems <u>impossible</u> for it to be the mechanism of divine, saving power.
- Whom does God use? How is His method so <u>different</u> from the standards of the world?
    1. Not the wise, influential or high <u>society</u>.
    2. He bypasses those who trust in themselves and their own <u>strength</u> and wisdom.
    3. He uses the <u>weak</u>, the lowly, the nobodies to shame the wise and the strong (1

Corinthians 1:26-29).
- The <u>message</u> itself is foolishness to the world, and its advocates – those of us viewed not as movers and shakers, not as influential or of high society but, rather, as the weak and lowly – are considered fools.

THE ARMY

- We are participating in a <u>battle</u> as warriors in an army (Ephesians 6:10-12).
- The army is described in 1 Corinthians 1:26-31 as having five categories of people: the foolish, the weak, the lowly, the despised and the nobodies. This is the way the world <u>views</u> us.
- Perhaps you have been thinking you were too unqualified for proclaiming and demonstrating the message of the cross? WRONG! You are <u>perfect</u> for this army. Step right up behind the fools.
- We are stronger and more invincible than any worldly way, for <u>hidden</u> within our contemptible exterior is the all-victorious presence of <u>Christ</u> and the irresistible power of the Holy Spirit.
- We may not look like much on the outside, but we are children of the Most High God! We are:
  1. "<u>Chosen</u>, adopted and sealed" (Galatians 1:4).
  2. God's "<u>workmanship</u>" (Ephesians 2:10).
  3. His temple, "<u>paid</u> for with His Son's blood" (1 Corinthians 3:16, 19-20).
  4. "<u>Heirs</u> of God and co-heirs with Christ" (Romans 8:17).
  5. Backed by God: "If God is <u>for</u> us, who can be against us?" (Romans 8:31).
  6. Indwelt by the Holy Spirit and His <u>gifts</u>.
  7. Given the <u>armor</u> of God.
  8. Prayed for by <u>Jesus</u>.
- Our only <u>weapon</u> is the message of the cross. This is a message about changed lives, healed bodies, restored families, a revolutionized nation and world.

PROCLAIMING THE MESSAGE

- The message of the cross is spoken in many places, but often it is merely preached - rendered in a <u>tiresome</u> manner where it is not asked for, nor wanted.
- We are called to do <u>more</u> than preach with words.
- We are called to proclaim this message and to <u>demonstrate</u> it by our lives. That is not tiresome!
- When people see that we are <u>doing</u> what we are saying, they will come.
- When there are signs and proofs of the kingdom of God - healing, salvation, the Spirit of God being poured out - people are seeing the Kingdom of God <u>breaking</u> into the kingdom of darkness (Colossians 1:13).
- When we tell people about the message of the cross and do not <u>demonstrate</u> the power of that message by praying for the sick, when we stifle the moving of the Holy Spirit through fear or ignorance, or when we do not teach the people of God how to do what Jesus did, we are walking in <u>disobedience</u>!
- If the Gospel is indeed Good News, then power must <u>accompany</u> the message.
- For 2,000 years, people have been asking the same questions and looking for something

<u>real</u> in their lives.

- They need to come to a point where they ask, "What is this you are saying and doing? Is this what God is like? Is this message the answer I am <u>looking</u> for? If this is real, tell me about Jesus!"
- Proclaiming and demonstrating this message is what we are called to do as children of God.
- Before this can happen, we need to do three "foolish" things:
    1. Place Jesus back on the <u>throne</u> of our lives.
    2. Spend time with God building intimacy through worship, Scripture, solitude and silence. He must become our dearest <u>friend</u>.
    3. Understand what He has called you to do – be <u>Jesus</u> to the world – and do it!

Discussion questions for this chapter are on page 61

7

WHEN IT IS OKAY TO BE A CHILD

The introduction to this chapter explores the concept of childlikeness, which is the <u>pathway</u> to intimacy. Childlikeness involves humility, trust, openness, eagerness, and a recognition of "one's nothingness, expecting everything from the good God" (Therese of Lisieux).

THE HONESTY OF CHILDREN

- Children have no problem realizing their <u>limitations</u>.
- Children can be trifling, fickle, uncooperative, bored, and spoiled, but they can also be incredibly <u>honest</u> and trusting.
- Jesus refers to the open, trusting and unashamed aspects of childlikeness when he talks about <u>humbling</u> oneself like a little child (Matthew 18:3,4).
- When Jesus says it is easier "for a camel to go through the eye of a needle than for a *rich* man to <u>enter</u> the kingdom of God " (Matthew 19:24), one could just as easily insert the word *proud*, or *distrustful*, *apathetic* or *fearful* in place of the word rich. Those are all aspects of "grown-up", un-childlike attitudes.
- If you are prepared to be as <u>open</u>, enthusiastic, honest and trusting as little children, you can enter the kingdom of heaven.

THE SENSITIVITY AND OPENNESS OF CHILDREN

- Jesus: "Let the children alone, and do not hinder them from coming to Me; for the kingdom of heaven <u>belongs</u> to such as these" (Matthew 19:13-15).
- The children heard the same words as the adults, but they heard, believed and accepted.

They were open to <u>receive</u>, not analyze.

- Jesus knew that, though far from innocent, the children were more <u>sensitive</u> to the supernatural world than adults tend to be. Often what adults regard as ordinary things are considered by children to be matters of great <u>significance</u>.
- My granddaughter: "Look at the pretty roses God made for <u>us</u>!"
- Our childlike <u>enthusiasm</u> may have been dulled to such a degree that we no longer enjoy the wonder of God's creation.

RETAINING CHILDLIKE QUALITIES

- Jesus is not encouraging us to be child*ish*, but to retain the <u>child*like*</u> qualities of honesty, sensitivity and openness when we grow up so that we can be <u>receptive</u> to what the Father says and does.
- Anonymous: "A child is <u>dependent</u> and trusting – at least until adult unworthiness breaks the trust. A child is <u>friendly</u> and unconscious of status or race – until adult prejudice spoils that relationship. A child is <u>candid</u>...A child lives in constant wonder...A child <u>expects</u> great things of life and finds them."

BEING CHILDLIKE: A DOORWAY INTO RELATIONSHIP

- Brennan Manning: "The <u>positive</u> qualities of a child – openness, trusting dependence, playfulness, simplicity, sensitivity to feelings – restrain us from <u>closing</u> ourselves off to new ideas,...the surprises of the Spirit and risky opportunities for growth."
- When we rediscover that we are the <u>beloved</u>, we also re-take our childlike innocence. We are aware of our core identity and we refuse to be intimidated by people who prevent us from being <u>real</u>.
- Until we break out of the mold created by the expectations of others, we will not become childlike in our <u>wonder</u> of God and His creation, nor will we grasp what He has done for us personally.
- A.W. Tozer: "For <u>me</u> Christ died...And when He arose on the third day it was for me; and when He poured out upon the disciples the promised Holy Spirit it was that He might continue in me the work He had been doing for <u>me</u> since the morning of creation."
- Becoming like a child is like a doorway to our <u>union</u> with God.
- It means going <u>deep</u> emotionally, being sensitive, being spiritually connected and knowing that we are His beloved and are held by Him.

THINGS THAT KEEP US FROM CHILDLIKENESS

- *Not Understanding the Father's Love*
    1. He loves you as much as He loves His <u>Son</u> Jesus!
    2. This is <u>hard</u> to grasp because we see ourselves as weak sinners full of evil, ugly things.
    3. But He forgave ALL our sins. His death for us as sinners shows His *agape*

(<u>unconditional</u>) love for us (Romans 5:8).

- *Holding Back our Emotions*
  1. God not only has agape love for us, He has *phileo* love (a love that touches, that has <u>feelings</u>).
  2. Some of us have a difficult time expressing feelings due to gender expectations, past experiences that have shut down our feelings, or <u>fear</u> of rejection.
  3. As adults we tend to see God at a distance, but children have no problem running up to someone and saying, "I want to sit on your <u>lap</u>."
  4. Our emotions were created as a part of our <u>basic</u> makeup.
  5. We <u>need</u> His affectionate touch, affirming words and blessing, for these are healing to our souls.
- *Not Having the Heart of a Child*
  1. Central to receiving affection is a heart turned <u>toward</u> God in childlike trust (See 1 Samuel 16:7).
  2. The heart is the <u>center</u> of the spiritual nature of man, the center of powerful emotions, enthusiasm, sexual desire, the seat of love and hatred, of feelings and affections that can range from joy to terror.
  3. When we can be childlike in our hearts we understand that it is <u>okay</u> to feel and express emotion.
- *Not Understanding the Human Jesus*
  1. We can become so focused on His divinity that we can miss His <u>humanity</u>.
  2. John leaned his head on the <u>heart</u> of God (John 13:23,25).
  3. Children look <u>beyond</u> the outer man to see the heart.
  4. Jesus came to show us the heart of the Father, and the Father's heart <u>hungers</u> to have time with us.
  5. When we <u>wait</u> on Him and minister to Him we can hear and know what is on His heart.

ADOPTED BY GOD

- God promises an inheritance to those who come to Jesus as little children. The inheritance is a result of our <u>adoption</u>, which is a result of His grace (See Ephesians 1:5).
- An adopted child receives the <u>same</u> benefits and standing as would a natural child.
- From Romans 8:14-17: "You received the Spirit of *sonship* [other translations say *adoption*]. And by Him we cry, 'Abba, Father.'...we are God's <u>children</u>...we are heirs – heirs of God and co-heirs with Christ."
- Adoption gives us <u>access</u> to an intimate relationship with God as our "Abba" Father. "Abba" was the word used familiarly by children talking to their fathers – a word much like our words *Daddy* or *Papa*.
- From Dr. Martin Lloyd Jones: "Spirit of adoption" means not merely a *belief* of the fact that we have been adopted into God's family, but a consciousness of it, a <u>feeling</u> of it.
- This adoption gives us access to Him, but we must also give Him access to <u>us</u>.
- When we truly grasp that we are <u>valuable</u> members of God's family and that God loves us as much as He loved Jesus, we will want to hang out with Him.
- When the reality of this love came to me – A healing conference in the late 1980's. "God, how much do you love me?" "<u>This</u> much," said God, showing His open palms with wounds in them.

- 1 John 3:1: "How great is the love the Father has <u>lavished</u> on us."

COMING AS A LITTLE CHILD

- The Kingdom belongs to those who are trusting, dependent and <u>expectant</u>.
- As we begin to take on these childlike qualities we will move into a place where we too will want to waste time with God simply because we <u>enjoy</u> being with Him.

Discussion questions for this chapter are on page 62

8

THE TRAPS OF CONDEMNATION, INTIMIDATION AND ACCUSATION

The introduction to this chapter lays out a sequence necessary for intimacy with God to begin. Forgiveness leads to freedom from the traps of condemnation, intimidation and accusation. Freedom from these traps will lead to more complete openness, honesty, vulnerability, trust and intimacy with God.

WE ARE FORGIVEN!

- Ephesians 1:7: "In Him we have redemption through His blood, the forgiveness of <u>sins</u>" (See also Colossians 1:13-14).
- This fact is hard to understand and <u>accept</u>.
- According to William Shannon, many of us believe in a caricature of God, "someone who is gracious to me when I am good, but who <u>punishes</u> me relentlessly when I am bad. This is not the God whom Jesus called 'Abba.'"
- The scene with John resting his head on Jesus' chest (John 13:13-25) sends a powerful message to us individually and corporately.
- Brennan Manning: "The beloved disciple sends a message both to the <u>sinner</u> covered with shame and to the local <u>church</u> tentative and slow to forgive for fear of appearing lax or liberal. The number of people who have fled the church because it is too patient or compassionate is negligible; the number who have fled because they find it too <u>unforgiving</u> is tragic."

WE ARE TO FORGIVE

- In addition to being forgiven by God, we are to forgive <u>others</u>, even those who have hurt us deeply (See Matthew 5:43-44).
- But we feel that if we forgive someone, it lets the person "off the <u>hook</u>" too easily.
- But scripture is clear: "Forgive as the Lord forgave you" (Colossians 3:13 and Ephesians 3:32).
- Unforgiveness gives Satan ground in our lives and causes <u>us</u> - not the person we cannot forgive – to <u>suffer</u>.
- Often, the person who is responsible is not <u>affected</u> in any way and may not even be aware that he or she has hurt us.
- Mike's story of the close friend he wouldn't forgive: I was beginning to draw back and did not want to be around him…God made it clear that I had not forgiven him. I quickly forgave him and asked God to forgive me for holding that <u>anger</u> inside…I knew I was <u>healed</u> from this anger when I saw my friend the next time.
- Two <u>reasons</u> why it is important that we forgive
    1. We are warned to forgive so that Satan cannot take <u>advantage</u> of us (2 Corinthians 2:10-11).
    2. We are <u>required</u> to forgive (Matthew 6:14, 15).
- The parable of the unforgiving servant (Matthew 18:23-35) – The unforgiving servant was turned over to the jailers, the <u>tormentors</u>! In other words, unforgiveness turns us over to torment by guilt, shame, anger, fear or bitterness.
- Unforgiveness is a <u>prison</u>!
- Often we must forgive <u>ourselves</u>. If we have caused a lot of pain and difficulty for ourselves because of our own choices and responses, it is necessary to forgive ourselves and release our loads of guilt and shame into His flow of mercy and <u>grace</u>.

I DESERVE CONDEMNATION!

- To <u>condemn</u> means "to pronounce judgment against or to declare unfit for use."
- It is one of three traps <u>Satan</u> uses to keep us from intimacy with God.
- Story of the woman caught in adultery (John 8:1-11)
    1. In front of a large crowd, the Pharisees put before Jesus a woman they had caught in adultery. "The <u>law</u> of Moses says to stone her," they said. "What do you say?"
    2. Jesus: "Let those who have <u>never</u> sinned throw the first stones."
    3. The accusers went away, beginning with the oldest, until the woman was left with Jesus.
    4. Jesus turned to her. "Where are your accusers? Did not even one of them <u>condemn</u> you?"
    5. "Neither do I. Go and sin no more."
- Suddenly she was free from condemnation, but now she was faced with some <u>choices</u>.
    1. She could decide to not accept the forgiveness and become an easy <u>target</u> for Satan, who would keep her trapped under condemnation.
    2. She could decide to <u>not</u> forgive her accusers or release them from what they had done to her. Bitterness, anger and resentment would have set in and kept her under condemnation.

- Condemnation is often brought about by <u>words</u> spoken to us by people who are significant in our lives. Their words are like daggers driven into our hearts: "You'll never amount to anything," etc.
- If we believe those people and accept their statements as <u>true</u>, they can be the very words that condemn us to becoming losers and failures.
- If we <u>think</u> we are condemned, then we <u>act</u> like we are condemned and we never experience the lavish love the Father wants to pour out on us because we believe we do not <u>deserve</u> it.
- Instead, we must see ourselves as God sees us – forgiven, pure, holy and His beloved. This is a result of seeing God as He is <u>revealed</u> in Jesus.
- Francis Frangipane: "The ultimate purpose behind revelation is that what we <u>behold</u>, we are to become."

INTIMIDATION CAN KEEP YOU DOWN!

- To <u>intimidate</u> means "to fill with fear, to coerce, inhibit or discourage by or as if by threats."
- This is another trap that the <u>enemy</u> uses to block us from intimacy with God.
- Intimidation keeps us from honesty with ourselves and with others. <u>Fear</u> of rejection pervades one's whole life.
- Brennan Manning: "...to disclose our dark <u>secrets</u> to another is intolerably risky."
- Our enemy has been so successful at backing us into a corner that we not only fear honesty with others, but we <u>hide</u> all our secret sins and vanities from God, which is the height of absurdity.
- Intimidation <u>keeps</u> us from deep intimacy with anyone and tragically <u>stops</u> us from laying bare our soul to God, which prevents us from receiving forgiveness for those very things that God will use in us to bless others.

ACCUSATION IS DEADLY!

- <u>Accusation</u> means bringing charges against someone.
- Satan is the <u>accuser</u>. We hear him say, "You are nothing. You are of no value to God. How can you be a Christian and do that?"
- This is the third <u>trap</u> Satan uses to block our intimacy with the Father.
- Mikes' story of his ministry being misunderstood and <u>accused</u> of being unscriptural and leaning toward New Age beliefs
    1. We were deeply <u>hurt</u>.
    2. I found myself becoming angry and resentful.
    3. "God, why is this happening when all I want to do is pray for people!"
    4. We were so focused on the opposition that we were <u>distracted</u> from what God had clearly called us to do.
    5. We began to have <u>doubts</u> in our minds that maybe what we were doing was wrong.
    6. We were worried about having to <u>defend</u> ourselves.
    7. Many people left the church.
    8. Satan <u>used</u> this situation to manipulate, divide and destroy people.

9. I had to pray through some <u>unforgiveness</u> issues with people who had hurt me.
10. In forgiving these people, I pulled the <u>ground</u> from under Satan. The very things of which Satan was accusing me – anger, bitterness, etc. – I <u>released</u> to God.
11. If I had allowed Satan to keep me in this <u>trap</u>, Wholeness Ministries may very well have been destroyed.

- Mike's story of Satan's accusations regarding his father
    1. I was 18 when my father died as a result of a beating outside a bar.
    2. Because there was not enough evidence to bring this case to trial the court <u>dropped</u> the charges against the men who had beaten my father.
    3. I felt <u>betrayed</u> by the judicial system and was angry at the police, sheriff, attorneys and judge.
    4. This planted in me seeds of <u>anger</u>, rebellion and distrust against any <u>authority</u>, especially the legal system.
    5. I was also angry with my father; his death was his own fault.
    6. I felt abandoned and <u>lonely</u> without him.
    7. I was also angry with God.
    8. Because I did not want to risk getting hurt again, I would not <u>let</u> God love me deeply or intimately, and I found it difficult to allow other men close relationally, making most of my relationships <u>superficial</u>.
    9. Many years later, I finally <u>faced</u> the pain and God was able to come in and heal the wounds.
    10. I accepted God's love and let others get <u>close</u> to me.
    11. I forgave those involved in this incident and was able to get on with my life and move into an <u>intimate</u> relationship with God.
    12. Before that I had given the enemy ample <u>ammunition</u> to accuse me.
- Satan stands before God at any opportunity to accuse us, and he takes every <u>opportunity</u> we give him when we hold on to unforgiveness.

TO FORGIVE OR NOT TO FORGIVE

- The <u>decision</u> to forgive causes us to experience freedom and release from sin.
- Otherwise we remain <u>trapped</u> under condemnation, intimidation and accusation.
- These traps keep us from spending time with God and from developing a <u>relationship</u> with Him that is rewarding and freeing.

Discussion questions for this chapter are on page 63

9

WHAT ARE YOU WILLING TO DIE FOR?

The introduction to this chapter points out that in our culture, most people don't worship physical idols as you would see in the East, but instead we spend an inordinate amount of time and attention pursuing the <u>gods</u> of wealth, appearance and education. When made our top <u>priorities</u>, these idols keep us from spending time with God.

OUR CULTURAL IDOLS

- It is easy for us to fill our lives with things that become the very idols God wants to <u>destroy</u>.
- In fact, idols <u>clutter</u> our lives.
- Francis Frangipane: [An idol] "is something that rules us and makes us its slave. For some, fear is an idol; for others it is lust…Whatever challenges Jesus' right to our <u>hearts</u> becomes an enemy to Him, which He will confront."
- Three major idols in our culture
  1. Fast-paced Society
     a. We are slaves to its <u>frantic</u> pace.
     b. We expect everything to happen quickly.
     c. We are <u>driven</u> to succeed.
     d. We have lost an appreciation for <u>stillness</u> and solitude.
  2. Religion
     a. We look <u>down</u> on others whose belief systems or ways of worship are not like ours.
     b. Our image of God is in our <u>minds</u>, but not in our hearts.

  c. Instead of looking down on others, we should be looking <u>up</u> at God with gratefulness.

  d. Our "religious knowledge" may pacify us in our anxious striving, but it will not fill our lives with the fullness of God that brings true <u>peace</u>.

 3. Intellectual Knowledge

  a. Our self-made intellectual understanding of God is like having "God in a <u>box</u>."

  b. Blaise Pascal: "God made man in His own image, and man returned the compliment."

  c. We think we know God and can therefore love God when He <u>fits</u> our image.

  d. But is it possible to love God when we only know <u>about</u> Him?

  e. With our finite minds can we understand the infinite?

  f. God: "To whom will you compare me or count me equal? (Isaiah 46:5)

  g. We may assume that God exists and thinks as we do, but we should really desire to know Him for who He <u>truly</u> is.

- Whatever the idols in our lives, we are <u>foolish</u> to create them and to worship them.
- What could possibly be so valued that we would <u>sacrifice</u> intimacy with the true God to pursue it?
- Idols create a <u>chasm</u> between us and God.

SHADRACH, MESHACH AND ABEDNEGO

- It is costly to <u>refuse</u> to worship cultural and personal idols.
- The Story of Shadrach, Meshach and Abednego in Daniel 3

 1. Who they were

  a. Three Jews who were <u>captured</u> when Jerusalem was conquered by the Babylonians.

  b. Brought to Babylon to serve the King in high positions.

  c. Known for their intelligence, integrity and <u>faithfulness</u> to their God.

 2. What happened to them

  a. Some leaders in the Babylonian government were <u>jealous</u> of them because the King had favored them.

  b. The leaders set up a plan – to <u>tattle</u> on the Jews to the King when they refused to worship the King's image even though the King had commanded that all the people must worship his statue or <u>die</u>.

  c. The three Jews did <u>not</u> worship the statue and the government leaders let the King know this.

  d. The King gave the three another chance, but still they <u>refused</u>.

  e. Perhaps the king's intentions were: "Look, I know you are believers in the Hebrew God and I really respect that and want to stay on good terms with you, but there's just this <u>one</u> <u>thing</u> that you've got to do, because if you don't it makes me look bad. If I let you get away with this, then anybody else can challenge my authority."

  f. But they still refused to <u>compromise</u> their belief in God, so the King ordered that the three Jews be <u>thrown</u> into a furnace.

  g. The flames of the furnace killed the men who threw the Jews into the furnace.

h. As the King looked into the furnace, he saw four men, not three, and all were unbound and <u>walking</u> in the middle of the fire. The fourth man had the "appearance of a god."
i. The King called them out.
j. Not one part of their bodies or clothing were even singed by the fire.
k. The King <u>praised</u> the Hebrew God and the three men (See Daniel 3:19-30).

- *The Significance of this Story*
  1. It is about faith and <u>trust</u>, no matter what the cost.
  2. It is about <u>obedience</u>. They were obedient to the point of death.
  3. They were faced with two <u>temptations</u>, the same we face today.
     a. Perversion – to be directed <u>away</u> from what is right. If they could be distracted, they could be perverted. Idolatry is a perversion of a desire to see God.
     b. Compromise – If they wanted to maintain their positions of political <u>power</u>, they would have to compromise.
  4. Nobody else was bothered about bowing down before the idol.
     a. It is doubtful that everyone else bowed down to the idol because they loved the King; they probably fell down because they didn't want to <u>die</u>.
     b. They didn't have the conviction to <u>stand</u> for what they believed.
  5. These men were demonstrating with their <u>actions</u> that they believed what they spoke with their mouths.
     a. They <u>agreed</u> that what they were accused of was true.
     b. They did not try to <u>defend</u> themselves.
     c. Dead or alive, they knew they were in God's <u>hands</u>.
     d. Their understanding of the nature of God led to a fear and <u>awe</u> of Him that caused them to be willing to die rather than serve pagan gods.
     e. They must have spent a significant amount of <u>time</u> <u>with</u> <u>God</u> to possess the qualities that caused them to face death rather than turn to idolatry.
     f. The proof of the power of their God was not demonstrated until <u>after</u> they were tossed in the fire.
- Have you ever been in a situation where you knew God was <u>able</u> to rescue you, but you were not sure He would? Were you willing to go on, regardless of the cost?
- We may spend years walking with God, growing into a deep relationship with Him before our faith is tested. But when the <u>test</u> comes, because of our <u>relationship</u> with the Lord, we can stand strong and unwavering.

WE MUST DIE TO OUR IDOLS

- Anything that stands between us and a deep, intimate walk with God cannot be politely tolerated. We have a <u>jealous</u> God (See Exodus 34:14).
- God's jealousy is not like petty, possessive and insecure human jealousy; God's jealousy is based on His pure <u>love</u> for us.
- Richard Foster: "Today the heart of God is an open <u>wound</u> of love. He aches over our distance and <u>preoccupation</u>. He mourns that we do not draw near to Him. He grieves that we have forgotten Him. He weeps over our obsession with muchness and manyness. He <u>longs</u> for our presence."
- We must be willing to <u>die</u> to those values that have first place in our hearts.

- Brennan Manning makes the case that we are <u>imposters</u>: Pretend you are smart around the well-educated, rich around the wealthy, religious around the spiritual, etc. "The pursuit of money, power, glamour, sexual prowess, recognition and status enhances one's self-importance and creates the illusion of success."
- All of these imposter motives are actually <u>idols</u> that separate us from knowing God.
- To allow anything – especially any idols – to keep us from time with God is to <u>miss</u> the very reason God created us.

Discussion questions for this chapter are on page 64

10

THE KIND OF PERSON GOD USES

The introduction to this chapter makes two points that are developed in the next few pages: To be used by God, we need to spend significant time with Him, and spending time with Him will result in life <u>changes</u> that transform us into the kind of person God uses.

CONFRONTING THE REALITY OF JESUS CHRIST

- Rather than just another layer of religious information, there should be a lifestyle change that brings us into the truth and <u>reality</u> of God.
- Francis Frangipane: "On the road to Damascus, Paul was not blinded and devastated by a 'new doctrine' – he met the reality of Jesus Christ! When John beheld our glorified Lord on Patmos, it was not a 'new spiritual insight' that left him slain as a dead man – he beheld Jesus Christ!"
- Change in both thinking and attitude requires a <u>lifetime</u>, not just attending a seminar or reading a book. It requires that we face who we are and what radical changes need to be made to bring us to where we are totally committed to being the men or women God can use.

WHAT IS YOUR LIFE OBJECTIVE?

- Mike's story of working for a man whose life's objective was to make as much <u>money</u> as possible.
    1. The man said, "I do not <u>need</u> God. I have everything I want – money, power and possessions. He can't give me anything I don't already have."

2. A few weeks later the man <u>died</u> in a plane crash.
3. God: "Michael, is this what you <u>want</u> to give your life to acquiring?"
4. I realized that those things to which I had attached such importance were of <u>little value</u> to me, to my family or to God.
5. It was the beginning of some <u>radical</u> changes in my life objectives.

- What we choose to do for a living must never be our life objective, because it is only <u>temporary</u>!
- If we seek Him, <u>He</u> will assume responsibility for meeting every need in our lives.
- Paul speaks of the tremendous <u>potential</u> in the life of one man in 2 Timothy 2:2. Mike's paraphrase: "You teach to faithful men the things that I have taught you and if they will do likewise this message will multiply beyond your wildest imagination!"
- When we embark on the quest to know God, allowing Him to release the individual potential He invested in each of us, our life objectives will <u>change</u>.
- We will experience the wonderful freedom of dependence on God and the freedom from dependence on <u>man</u>.

WE MUST BE WILLING TO PAY THE PRICE

- This journey must become your passion, but this passion will be <u>costly</u>. It cost Jesus His life.
- Brennan Manning: "The four evangelists do not spare us the brutal details of the losses Jesus suffered for the sake of integrity, the price He paid for fidelity to His <u>passion</u>, His person and His mission."
- All that you value must be held with an <u>open</u> hand. God must be free to do with you and take from you as He pleases.
- Should you not be able to trust Him with everything if His love for you is <u>perfect</u>?
- The story of Joseph, earthly father of Jesus (Matthew 1 and 2).
  1. He was faced with the <u>tough</u> situation of his fiancée being pregnant even though they had not had sexual relations.
  2. God: "I want you to marry Mary." Joseph <u>did</u>.
  3. After Jesus was born, God said: "Go to Egypt." Joseph <u>did</u>.
  4. God told Him to return to Israel and settle in Nazareth. Joseph <u>did</u>.
- Each of these decisions was <u>costly</u> for Joseph. But He was willing to pay any price to have the will of God fulfilled in his life.
- Joseph's willingness to pay the costly price in his own life enabled God to bring the <u>salvation</u> of mankind to all of us.
- Joseph's priority was in the right place. His relationship with the Father came <u>first</u>.

CHANGES ALONG THE JOURNEY

- As you spend time with God in your transformation <u>journey</u>, a number of things will happen.
- *Developing A Love for The Word* – St. Jerome: "The Scriptures are shallow enough for a babe to come and drink without fear of drowning, and <u>deep</u> enough for theologians to swim in without ever touching bottom."
- *Producing the Heart of a Servant* – Jesus even washed the feet of Judas, the one who would betray Him (John 13). We must learn the concept of leading by <u>serving</u>.

- *Becoming Part of God's Team* – Spending time with God will cure you of having an independent spirit. You are part of a temple, where you and others are being built <u>together</u> (See Ephesians 2:19-21).
- *Losing Confidence in the Flesh* – Francis Frangipane: "In time, we discover that all true strength, all true effectiveness…begins with discovering our <u>need</u>…As the outer shell of self-righteousness crumbles, Jesus Himself becomes God's answer to every man who cries for holiness and power in his walk."
- *Loving People* – Jesus: "Love each other as I have loved you" (John 15:12). Look at the love He demonstrated: He was patient, encouraging, incredibly trusting even to Judas. Imagine His love toward the adulterous woman, or to lepers, whom He actually <u>touched</u>.
- *Confronting Sin and Bitterness* – God will bring to remembrance areas of anger or bitterness that He wants you to face. He will require you to make <u>peace</u> with all men and to allow <u>no</u> sin to go unchallenged in your life (Hebrews 12:14-15).
- *Seeking Discipline* – The gold medal goes to the athlete who has worked hard, who has learned how to discipline himself, who has learned to say <u>no</u> to the many distractions around him, who has a clear cut objective and has <u>resolved</u> to stay in it. This is the kind of person God uses (See 1 Corinthians 9:24-27).

OUR FOUNDATION IS CHRIST

- You may be saying, "Hey, I am pretty useful to God. I am a Christian, I go to church, I pay my tithe, and I give a little time now and then to help out with church work. Everything is good, right?" Wrong!
- 1 Corinthians 3:11-15 describes the folly of <u>starting</u> out with the foundation of Christ, but building on that foundation with the <u>wrong</u> things, symbolized by wood, hay and straw. "The fire will test the quality of each man's work. If what he has built survives, he will receive his reward. If it is burned up, he will suffer loss; he himself will be saved, but only as one escaping through the flames."
- What are you going to do when you face Jesus with your hands full of ashes from building your life with wood, hay and straw?
- What if He were to say to you, "Let me take you into this room and show you what your life could have been like if only you had done what I asked, if only you had been faithful to Me, if only you had disciplined your life and made it really <u>count</u>, as I wanted you to do."

WE ARE THE TREASURE!

- Matthew 13:44-46: "The kingdom of heaven is like treasure hidden in a field. When a man found it, he hid it again, and then in his joy went and sold <u>all</u> he had and <u>bought</u> that field."
- This parable is drenched with <u>meaning</u>.
- The man in the field symbolizes <u>Jesus</u>. He wants us to realize that we are His inheritance. <u>We</u> are the treasure in the field. He <u>gave</u> His all for us to have relationship with Him now and to eventually live in heaven with Him.
- Lloyd Ogilvie: "Where can he get the money to buy the field? Caution and discretion fly out the window! He sells <u>everything</u> he owns."
- Jesus gave up everything He had. He <u>gave up</u> His place with the Father to come and

spend 33 years with us.

- From the world's perspective those 33 years were a <u>failure</u>, and if we do not grasp that we are God's treasure, then we ourselves also see them as years of failure.
- When we spend prolonged periods of prayer and solitude with <u>Him</u>, then we begin to <u>understand</u> that we are His treasure, and that we are significant, accepted and secure.
- Then we will surrender our hearts totally to Him and His will becomes the passionate <u>purpose</u> of our lives.
- Lloyd Ogilvie: "When we realize we are the treasure for whom Christ died, we will treasure doing His <u>will</u> at all costs!"

Discussion questions for this chapter are on page 65

11

OUR GOAL IS INTIMACY

The introduction to this chapter states that true <u>worship</u> leads to intimacy with God. Mike says that worship is not just talking or singing about God, but expressing love <u>to</u> God. It includes deep feeling and tenderness. Our goal in worship is to <u>know</u> Him better, to touch Him, and to be consumed by His Presence, and this results in intimacy with Him.

CREATED FOR A PURPOSE

- God <u>created</u> human beings to worship Him.
- <u>All</u> of creation was made to worship God (See Psalm 148:1-12).
- A.W. Tozer: "All else fulfills its <u>design</u>; flowers are still fragrant and lilies are still beautiful, …the birds still sing with their thousand-voice choir…and the sun and the moon and the stars all move on their rounds doing the will of God." But where is man in all of this?
- As a result of the Fall, we do not worship in the way God <u>meant</u> for us to worship. We describe worship in terms of what we <u>receive</u> from it, not fully understanding that worship is not about us. It is about God.
- Much of our worship has become a <u>performance</u> that is rooted in fear and pride.
- Yet God yearns for us to worship Him, because He wants so badly for us to be <u>restored</u> to that place of intimate communion.

SPIRIT TO SPIRIT

- Jesus to the Samaritan woman: "We must worship in <u>spirit</u> and in truth" (John 4:19-24).
- Deep inside every one of us dwells the essence of our being – our spirit. It is the sum total of who we are. It is what makes each of us <u>unique</u>.
- 1 Corinthians 2:11: "For who among men knows the <u>thoughts</u> of a man except the man's spirit within him? In the same way no one knows the thoughts of God except the Spirit of God."
- A.W. Tozer: "[Man is] a spirit having a body. That which makes him a <u>human</u> being is not his body but his <u>spirit</u>, in which the image of God originally lay."
- John 4:23: "The time is coming and is already here when true worshippers will worship the Father in spirit and in truth. The Father is <u>looking</u> for anyone who will worship Him that way."
- Imagine your spirit <u>connected</u> with the Spirit of God while involved in worship. A.W. Tozer calls this "the union of the spirit of man with the Spirit of God."
- The slumbering spirit
    1. Described by John and Paula Sanford in *Healing the Wounded Spirit*: "If a baby growing from infanthood into childhood does not receive enough human touch, to that degree his spirit is not kept <u>awake</u> nor drawn forth into full functioning ability."
    2. This condition can result in feeling spiritually <u>disconnected</u> from God, like you are just going through the motions, but not emotionally attached to Him at all.
    3. The God of the Scriptures seems <u>distant</u>, judgmental or uncaring.
    4. Two kinds of slumbering spirits
        a. "Those who have <u>never</u> been drawn forth to life."
        b. "Those who did receive …nurture… but <u>turned away</u> from worship,…prayer and affection until their spirits fell asleep."
    5. In both kinds, "the heart is usually <u>hardened</u> as well" and both are the result of poor nurture or <u>neglect</u>, either by family or later on by one's self.
- Mike's summary of the Sandfords' discussion of the spirit in *Waking the Slumbering Spirit* – The functions of our personal spirits in relating to God are to <u>feel</u> His presence in corporate worship and in private devotions, to experience <u>communication</u> with God and receive inspiration from God.

OUR SPIRITS NEED AWAKENING

- When your spirit is fully awakened you can <u>connect</u> emotionally with God, and love and cherish what is in another person even more than your own <u>life</u>.
- Story of General Schwarzkopf in Vietnam
    1. The General and his men found themselves in the middle of a <u>minefield</u>.
    2. A soldier stepped on a mine and seriously injured his leg. He kept thrashing about, making the situation even more dangerous.
    3. The General knew he <u>needed</u> to go to the man and immobilize him, but this meant walking through a field of hidden mines.
    4. Schwarskopf: "I started through the minefield, one slow step at a time, staring at the ground, looking for telltale bumps or little prongs sticking up from the dirt…It seemed like a thousand years before I reached the kid."

5. The General got to the soldier and pinned him down. An engineer team helped the General and his men <u>out</u> of the minefield.

- General Schwarzkopf <u>valued</u> this man more than his own life. When your spirit is fully awake and connected to God's spirit, each person with whom you interact becomes a person of value to you. They are not just a bother, but a <u>creation</u> of God.
- True worship involves risk, and <u>change</u>.
- John Wimber: "If worship does not change us it has not been worship. In worship, resentments melt, and we experience an increased power, <u>compassion</u> and greater desire for obedience. Instead of worship becoming a special high or opiate, or escape, it drives us to respond, 'Here am I, <u>send me</u>' (Isaiah 6:8)."

WE NEED TO BE AVAILABLE

- Another reason why we miss connecting with God, in addition to slumbering spirits, is because of our <u>expectations</u>. The connection does not come in the form we think it should, so we are not fully available to hear, see or sense Him.
- From the poem *God Are You There?* (author unknown):
    The young man whispered, "God speak to me,"
    And a meadowlark sang, but the man did not hear…
    Then he looked around and said, "God let me see you,"
    And a star shone brightly, but the man did not notice…
    So the man cried out in despair, "Touch me God,
    And let me know you are there!"
    Whereupon God reached down and touched him,
    But the young man brushed the butterfly away
    And walked away unknowingly.
- If God is seeking, drawing and persuading us to come to Him, our responsibility is to be <u>available</u>. To be available is to <u>make time</u> to be with God.
- We have a responsibility to be in a <u>place</u> where God can seek and draw us, and where we can respond.

WORSHIPPING IN STILLNESS BEFORE GOD

- Singing, dancing, shouting, praying or reading the Word are all worship, but we must take time for <u>silence</u> and solitude if we are to go to the <u>depths</u> with God.
- It goes back to <u>waiting</u> on God.
- From Psalm 62:5-7: "Find <u>rest</u>, O my soul, in God alone; my hope comes from Him. He alone is my salvation; He is my fortress, I will not be shaken."
- Chuck Swindoll: "We grow and we learn – not when things come our way instantly, but when we are forced to <u>wait</u>. That's when God tempers and seasons us, making us mellow and <u>mature</u>."

WORSHIP HELPS US TO UNDERSTAND OUR WORTH

- Waiting allows me to get to in touch with my own <u>belovedness</u>.
- Brennan Manning: "When I allow God to <u>liberate</u> me from unhealthy dependence on people, I listen more attentively, love more unselfishly and am more compassionate and playful. I take myself less seriously, become aware that the breath of the Father is on my face and that my countenance is bright with laughter in the midst of an adventure I thoroughly enjoy."
- Anthony Padovano: "It means I don't figure out and don't analyze, but simply lose myself in the thought or the experience of just being alive... it's <u>good</u> to be there, even if I don't know where 'there' is, or why it's good to be there. Already I have reached a contemplative <u>stillness</u> in my being."
- Worship allows you to understand that it is God who has called you by <u>name</u> (See Isaiah 43:1,4 and Isaiah 53:10).
- In spending time with Him you are like a <u>child</u> on his Father's lap, His arms wrapped lovingly around you. You are resting in complete security and peace, knowing that in this place there is acceptance, protection and love.
- Francis Frangipane: [In this posture you should be able to] "continue day by day, and week by week, until you have drawn <u>near enough</u> to God that you can hear His voice, becoming confident that He is close enough to you to hear your whisper."

TRUE WORSHIP

- True worship involves the <u>total</u> personality – mind, emotions and will (Deuteronomy 6:5).
- Worship is not passive, but participative and <u>responsive</u>.
- It celebrates God and brings Him <u>pleasure</u>.
- When we truly worship we also <u>benefit</u>, just as you benefit when you do something for another human being. When you take a loved one out to dinner for a special evening, you do not sit there like a bump on a log, uninvolved. You are blessed because you are participating in a loving <u>act</u> of intimacy.
- Whether it is joyfully dancing or kneeling in reverence, worship is our <u>love</u> expressed <u>to</u> God, <u>for</u> God Himself.
- It is <u>not</u> a performance; it is an act of intimacy.
- It is my spirit <u>connecting</u> with His Spirit.
- The very idea that the Creator of the universe would even <u>permit</u> us to come into His presence should fill us with a sense of gratitude, awe and reverence.
- The God who created the universe, who heals the sick, who knows you need food and shelter to survive, against whom all military might is but a puff of dust, and beside whose power a swirling, raging river is but a trickle in the sand – THIS is the God <u>worthy</u> of our worship!

Discussion questions for this chapter are on page 66

12

THE REALITY OF GOD

The introduction to this chapter articulates the amazing fact that the God of the Universe wants each of us to spend time with Him so that He can <u>reveal</u> more of Himself to us and transform us into the image of Jesus. We are encouraged to not be distracted by merely adding another layer of religious knowledge or doctrine to our lives, but to head straight for the <u>reality</u> of God Himself.

A LIFE OF OBEDIENCE

- What an astonishing thought – a life of <u>complete</u> obedience without any reservations!
- What is freeing to me is that this life of obedience does not depend entirely on me; it must be a work of the <u>Spirit</u> within me.
- "I will let Him do this <u>in</u> me" is obedience. Not "I will do this."
- But we do have a <u>part</u> in the life of obedience. Our <u>responsibility</u> includes spending time with Him, setting aside all other responsibilities and activities to simply be with Him so we can achieve the intimacy He – and we – desire.
- Though the Spirit urges, invites and persuades, we must be in a place both physically and emotionally to <u>recognize</u> His prompting us to a deeper relationship with Him.
- If we are to live lives of obedience we must take seriously the words "Be <u>still</u> and know that I am God" (Psalm 46:10).
- To be still and wait may seem a daunting task, but once begun the task soon turns into a <u>journey</u> of adventure and expectancy – a journey that will take us into the presence of our Creator, a place from which we will not easily be pulled.

THE TRAP OF COMPLACENCY

- As we pursue our everyday lives, it is so easy to forget Who is calling us into relationship.
- How easily our daily routine blurs the reality of the Most Holy God waiting for us to notice Him. How easily we forget that God desires a genuine, intimate, bottom-of-our souls relationship with us.

HE REVEALS HIMSELF

- Once we are obedient to be still in His presence, He reveals Himself in a variety of ways:
    1. He brings peace that stills the busy mind and spirit.
    2. He brings physical relaxation.
    3. He speaks to us with thoughts of love whispered in our minds.
    4. Our spirits are connected with His and are refreshed and renewed.
    5. He reveals more of Himself in fresh ways through His Word.
    6. He reveals Himself through His creation.
    7. He speaks through the creations of others – the written word, a song or work of art.
- Whether you connect with God through His creation, the creation of others, or sitting quietly in an empty room, He will reveal Himself to you in ways He knows will speak to your individual heart.
- He asks only that you be still long enough to listen.

HE IS SO PROUD OF YOU!

- We might ask, "What is there to be proud of? I have never done anything significant."
- Brennan Manning writes from God's point of view: "Has it crossed your mind that I am proud you accepted the gift of faith I offered you? Proud that you freely chose me, after I had chosen you, as your Friend and Lord? Proud that with all your warts and wrinkles you haven't given up? Proud that you believe in me enough to try again and again?"
- Mike writes from God's point of view: "Do you know how it makes me feel that you want me? ...All the things you could be doing and you chose freely to spend time with me. I know you have sins and struggles. I know that you are not where you feel you need to be for me to love and accept you. But I still love you. And I am proud of you!"
- People who grew up in a home with loving parents have some understanding of what this means.
- Mike's story of one of his sons in the midst of serious rebellion
    1. "The problem is that you love me too much! Why can't you be like my friends' parents who don't care what they do?"
    2. He was frustrated because no matter what he did we never stopped loving him.
    3. It would have been much easier for him to rebel if we had simply rejected him. But we could not do that, and that love eventually paid off.
- Your Father God is proud of you because you are His and He loves you. Do not try to analyze, understand or "live up" to anything you think will make Him proud because it is not what you do but, rather, what you are. You are His.
- Believe it, accept it and live in the glorious freedom of it!

WHY NOT?

- If much of your journey with God consists of doing things <u>for</u> Him, then you are missing the best part of the journey.
- If you are tired of seeking approval in superficial relationships or working to live up to someone else's expectations, then get <u>alone</u> with God and just hang out.
- He wants to be with you. His heart longs for you! That is your <u>purpose</u> for being!
- The King of Kings, the Lord of Lords, our Creator and the Creator of all the universe is offering us the opportunity to spend as much <u>time</u> as we want with Him.
- We can worship Him, talk to Him, listen to Him and let Him love us. That should cause us to stand amazed.
- Why not allow yourself <u>permission</u> to just be with Him? Why not claim your place at His side?
- Why not <u>waste</u> some time with God!

Discussion questions for this chapter are on page 67

DISCUSSION QUESTIONS

1

WAITING AND WASTING

1. Before you read the first chapter, what expectations, or questions were raised in your mind by the term "wasting time with God"? How did the first chapter clarify, modify or answer these concerns?

2. Mike Evans quotes Edward Schillebeeckx, who said: "Failure to recognize the value of mere being with God, as the beloved, without doing anything, is to gouge the heart out of Christianity." If merely being with God, not doing anything, is the heart of Christianity, why do so few Christians take time to do it? Why don't YOU do it?

3. Which impediment to intimacy with God – "doing", fear of rejection, or walking in darkness – has been your greatest hindrance to time with God? What do you hope this book will help settle once and for all so that this hindrance no longer exists?

2

THE VALUE OF NURTURING THE SOUL

1. What evidence can you find in this chapter that proves how special you are to God. Why is Satan jealous of you?

2. Are there some truths you had never realized before that give you new hope that you do not need to struggle with issues of trust, rebellion, relationships, acceptance, shame, etc.? Explain.

3. Review the list under the section "Fighting the Battle". About which areas are you the most encouraged and eager to try?

3

THE BENEFITS OF WAITING ON GOD

1. This chapter develops the idea that the main benefits of waiting on God are provision of our needs, peace and rest. What kinds of things do you do, or do you see others do, to acquire provision for your needs, peace and rest *without* waiting on God?

2. In this chapter Mike discusses what silence is, why it is difficult, what can happen when we actually become silent in God's presence, and how he sits silently with God and his cup of coffee on many mornings. As you consider the prospect of silence with God, what aspects bother *you*? What aspects excite you? Explain.

4

ARE YOU LISTENING?

1. If the story of Balaam makes you think of a time you were sure you knew what God wanted you to do, and you are willing to share this with the group, tell what happened. Did you obey right away? Try to change God's mind as Balaam did? Need several gentle or not-so-gentle nudges from God to go the right way?

2. Re-read the section under "Discerning the Voice of God" that compares God's voice with Satan's voice (page 81, middle). What descriptive words were you not aware of before? Does any of this change how you will discern voices in the future?

3. If everyone in the group is in agreement to do this, try the Exercise in Listening to the Voice of God, described on page 83.

5

THE TRAGEDY OF THE CHURCH TODAY

1. Mike describes many church people as more concerned about growth and prosperity than the message of the cross, whose spiritual senses have been dulled to the point of being happy with the status quo, and who are afraid to go beyond what is normal into experiencing the extraordinary. Do you agree with Mike's observation? Where do you fit in this picture?

2. What is your response to the anonymous essay *Others May, You Cannot*, on pages 98 and 99? In what ways does it reveal the tragedy of the Church today, as Mike has discussed it? How close are you to choosing to stop merely following other Christians and moving into this "peculiar, personal, private, jealous guardianship and management of the Holy Spirit over your life"?

6

THE FOOLISHNESS OF GOD

1. The following statement is a response to one of Mike's main points in this chapter. Do you agree or disagree with it?

   The world sees the Christian message, beliefs and church activities as foolish. Even the Bible itself says the world sees it all as foolish. Yet, when you look at what the world offers to people in order to find peace, tranquility, healing and meaning, it turns out the other way around. *The world's* answers are foolish.

2. If you are a Christian, what convinced you that the message was true? If you are not a Christian, what would it take to convince you? Do you agree with what Mike says about people longing for something real?

3. If you are not "proclaiming and demonstrating this message", what do you think is keeping you from this? Which of the three things listed on page 112 are you hoping to resolve in your life so that you *can* proclaim and demonstrate the message?

7

WHEN IT IS OKAY TO BE A CHILD

1. What "grown-up" attitudes do you think have created walls between you and intimacy with God?

2. What single truth in this chapter gives you hope that it is not too late to become childlike in the Father's presence?

8

THE TRAPS OF CONDEMNATION, INTIMIDATION AND ACCUSATION

1. According to Mike, if you are having difficulty building intimacy with God, it may be because you are trapped by condemnation, intimidation and/or accusation. If you are in any of these traps, you are probably there because you have not yet accepted God's full forgiveness of you or you have not yet forgiven someone else. How do you think you fit in this picture? What are you beginning to understand to do about the things that are keeping you from intimacy with God?

2. How do Mike's stories of healing from his own unforgiveness encourage you to take similar steps?

9

What Are You Willing to Die For?

1. What is one concept or fact in the story of Shadrach, Meshach and Abednego that spoke to you in a new way? Explain.

2. Think of the kinds of cultural idols Mike discussed in this chapter and then re-read this quote from Richard Foster:

   "Today the heart of God is an open wound of love. He aches over our distance and preoccupation. He mourns that we do not draw near to Him. He grieves that we have forgotten Him. He weeps over our obsession with muchness and manyness. He longs for our presence."

   What do you believe God is saying to you personally right now, about the pursuits (i.e. idols) that tend to enslave you?

10

THE KIND OF PERSON GOD USES

1. If you have already begun spending intimate time with God, what changes discussed on pages 154-158 (a love for the Word, heart of a servant, etc.) have you already observed in your own thinking and attitude? How are you different from the way you used to be?

2. Did anything surprise you about Mike's discussion of the parable of the hidden treasure? Explain.

3. When Mike refers to discipline, do you think he is talking about working harder? Previously Mike has talked about waiting on God, resting, not taking yourself seriously, enjoying solitude, lessening of striving and increasing of peace. What do you think is the connection between discipline and waiting on God?

11

OUR GOAL IS INTIMACY

1. Describe a time when you know that you were *truly* worshipping God, when you knew your spirit was fully awake and connecting with God's Spirit, when it was good and it *felt* good to just be there, when you felt filled with more love and compassion than you normally had. Whether the setting was out in nature, in your car, in a church service or a small group or wherever, what do you think brought you into that true worship? How do you think you can recapture that intimacy with God on a regular basis?

2. Mike says that we have a responsibility to *be available, to be in a place* where God can seek and draw us, and where we can respond. What is this "place"? A location? A frame of mind? A block of time? Or all three and more?

3. How can you be in that place this week?

12

THE REALITY OF GOD

1. Mike writes, "If we are to live lives of obedience we must take seriously the words, 'Be still and know that I am God' (Psalm 46:10). What attitudes and actions would constitute taking these words *seriously*?

2. Does it surprise you that God is proud of you? Explain.

3. Mike's last sentence in the entire book is the last question to discuss: Why not waste some time with God? Can you think of any reason why *not*?

ABOUT WHOLENESS MINISTRIES

In 1989, Mike Evans founded Wholeness Ministries, a ministry whose two-fold purpose is to pray for healing and to train and equip others to pray for healing. This ministry of healing prayer is based on the mandate of Jesus Christ in Luke 4:18-19. We believe this mandate is to be carried out under the guidance and in the power of the Holy Spirit.

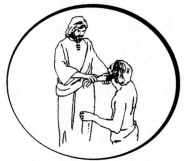

Mike is available for retreats, conferences and workshops. He and his team have taught and ministered extensively in Northern Ireland, England, Puerto Rico, Hungary, India and extensively throughout the United States. To schedule a Wholeness Ministries training conference, or to receive additional information, please contact:

P.O Box 80503
Bakersfield, California 93380 U.S.A
Phone: (661) 833-2920
Fax: (661) 833-2934
E-Mail: mevans@wholeness.org
www.wholeness.org

71

If You Like What You've Read...
Why Not Give It Away?

Share This Book:
Why Not Waste Time With God?

$14.95 (each) for one (plus shipping)
[To order just one, ask for Product #37]
$11.99 (each) for five (plus shipping)
[To order 5 ask for Product #38]
$9.99 (each) for ten (plus shipping)
[To order 10 ask for Product #39]

You can receive them in bulk directly from our ministry by calling 800-901-2025 ask for Product #39--a case of 10 at a 33% discount. OR ask for Product #38--a case of 5---still at a great savings.

Call 800-901-2025, and Ask for the Product Numbers Above Or Go To:
www.WasteTimeWithGod.org

How to Pray for Others with Tangible Results... the
Learning to Do What Jesus Did
Media Series

Product #40	**Prayer Team Ministry Training Book**

In *Learning To Do What Jesus Did*, you will discover unique approaches to praying for others. You will find a step-by-step plan for experiencing the healing power of Jesus in your ministry. After reading this book you will feel a new sense of freedom in praying for others. You will see wonderful, dynamic results as God uses you in exciting new ways to do the things Jesus did. This book will arm you with new knowledge, tools and confidence in praying effectively for yourself and others. As you will discover, learning to pray effectively is learning to follow Jesus.

Book • $18 (plus shipping)

Product #41	**9 Videotape Series**

This nine-tape video series is a must for pastors and lay ministers alike. It features approximately 10 hours of teaching from Michael and Jane Evans that will make ministering in the authority and power of Jesus easy to understand and exciting. Mike and Jane have taught this in many different denominations as well as several countries around the world. This series features the following tapes:

1) Introduction to Healing
2) A Healing Model
3) The Role of Faith
4) Authority of the Believer
5) Introduction to Inner Healing
6) Biblical Examples of Inner Healing
7) Forgiveness and Inner Healing
8) Deliverance
9) Spiritual Warfare

9 Valuable VHS Videos • $146 (plus shipping)

Product #42	**8 Audiotape Series**

This eight **audio** cassette series contains an edited version of the Learning to Do What Jesus Did Video Series (Product #41).

8 Audio Cassettes • $79 (plus shipping)

| Product #45 | **Wholeness Series (audio cassette)** |

OUR AUTHORITY TO BREAK CURSES AND SOUL TIES
People can be in bondage due to sin, soul ties and various types of curses. This teaching will explore the variety of ways we come under the influence of these curses and soul ties and how we have been given the authority through the Holy Spirit to break their influence over us.

DISCERNMENT
How do I know that it's God talking? What keys are there in recognizing the voice of God as opposed to the devil? This tape will teach some key ways we can understand and walk in discernment.

THE FATHER'S HEART
Many of us have barriers we've built which keep us from understanding the intimacy with which our Father God loves us. This is a crucial topic for our very survival in knowing our identity as sons and daughters of the King. We were made for intimacy with God. You're survival depends on it!

UNDERSTANDING YOUR AUTHORITY
When we understand spiritual authority, we will experience freedom in every part of our lives. It will happen when we recognize and use the gift of authority we have from God. We have this authority available to us today and we need to know how to operate in this authority.

ARE YOU LISTENING?
Often we go to God asking for His help or counsel. But then when God does try to speak to us we don't really want to hear what He has to say because we have our own agenda. This tape takes a hard look at what our real motivations are when we go to God seeking answers.

THOSE GIANTS ARE COMING DOWN
All of us have giants in our lives that strike fear into us, or they seem so huge we feel we will never overcome them. This exciting teaching brings into focus those qualities which can be inherent in our daily walk as believers, and which should characterize our response when we face those giants.

GOIN' FOR THE GOLD OR GOIN' FOR THE FURNACE
What are you willing to die for? We all give our lives to something. It may be our job, family, wealth, status, drugs, sex or material things. It is easy for these things to become idols and replace God in our lives. How do we identify and destroy them and put ourselves back in the place where God is truly Lord over our lives?

7 Audio Casettes • $35 (plus shipping)

Why Not Waste Time With God?
Help Others Reconnect With God

In addition to the book, we have made available an audio CD of Mike presenting a message about wasting time with God and the testimony of his personal journey.

If you would like to share this teaching with others, or use it to facilitate a group study, we are offering the following bulk packages at a discount:

- 4 "Why Not Waste Time With God Books (normally $14.95 each)
- 4 Audio CDs with the "Why Not Waste Time With God" Teaching (this CD is only available in this package)

When you order we will also enclose an extra book and CD for yourself as a bonus gift.

A $120 value for $75

**Call 800-901-2025, and Ask For
Product #36
Or Go To:
www.WasteTimeWithGod.org**

Printed in the United States
36545LVS00006B/7-16

9 781574 722376